Web 3 - Dec Web – The Complete Guide

Why Web3 Is The Internet of The Future

© Copyright Alex Anderson 2021 - All rights reserved.

The contents of this book may not be reproduced, duplicated, or transmitted without direct written permission from the author.

Under no circumstances will any legal responsibility or blame be held against the publisher for any reparation, damages, or monetary loss due to the information herein, either directly or indirectly.

Legal Notice:

You cannot amend, distribute, sell, use, quote, or paraphrase any part of the content within this book without the consent of the author.

Disclaimer Notice:

Please note the information contained within this document is for educational and entertainment purposes only. No warranties of any kind are expressed or implied. Readers acknowledge that the author is not engaging in the rendering of legal, financial, medical, or professional advice. Please consult a licensed professional before attempting any techniques outlined in this book.

By reading this document, the reader agrees that under no circumstances is the author responsible for any losses, direct or indirect, which are incurred as a result of the use of the information contained within this document, including, but not limited to, —errors, omissions, or inaccuracies.

Table of Contents

Introduction

Chapter 1: Why Do We Need a New Internet?

Chapter 2: What Is Web 3?
- *State Layer*
- *Computation Layer*
- *Component Layer*
- *Protocol Layer*
- *Scalability/Transfer Layer*
- *User Control Layer*
- *Application Layer*

Chapter 3: How Web 3 Works
- *Web 2 vs. Web 3 Architecture*
- **What Developers Should Know**
- *Other Challenges*

Chapter 4: Building a DApp
- *Let's Build a DApp*

Chapter 5: The Real Differences between Web 2 and Web 3
- **Centralization vs. Decentralization**

Chapter 6: The Main Features of Web 3
- *The Shift to Web 3*
- *The Web 3 Architecture*
- *How Will Web 3 Change Our Lives?*

Chapter 7: Why Web3 Is An Investment Opportunity

Chapter 8: 3 Most Promising Web3 Tokens for 2022

Conclusion

References

Introduction

Undoubtedly, one of the biggest revolutions in terms of technology is the Internet. We use it for just about everything these days, from communication to booking holidays, finding information to making purchases, and anything else you can think of.

That Internet is commonly known as Web2. While the Internet has been around for a long time, the revolution called Web2 has been here for less than two decades. Millions of communities have been created online in that time, global issues are widely debated via social media, and information comes at you from all directions. That is exactly what the Internet pioneers wanted. As Bill Gates once said, *"The internet is becoming the town square for the global village of tomorrow."*

Web2 allows for worldwide content distribution but perhaps its most important feature is that we can build on top of it, and that is where Web 3 comes in, the next generation of the Internet. In the same way Web2 began as a concept of using open networks to send information, Web 3 dives deeper and provides a transparent, fairer Internet and is, more often than not, associated with the blockchain.

In part, we can expect Web 3 to become more like a "web of data" that understands information, combines it, and automatically interprets it in a way that users gain an interactive experience. More than that, it will become a decentralized web, challenging the tech giants and their current dominance by taking the data and the power away from corporations and placing it squarely in the users' hands.

Why Is Web 3 Needed?

Whenever we do anything on the Internet, our data is copied and stored on a server by Facebook, Google, or any other major tech company we are using. That takes control of our data away from us. While it isn't necessarily bad to have third parties store our data, it starts to turn ugly when one entity is responsible for mediating everything.

Ask yourself this – do we really need a world where our data can be used out of malice or greed for nefarious purposes? This isn't about data privacy. It's about control. Every day, we give petabytes of data to others because we don't appear to have a choice. Even after you finish this book, you will continue to sign up to websites and apps, handing over your information just because it's convenient. After all, isn't that one of the benefits of technology?

Putting it into this context, the blockchain can drive the next-generation Internet by solving three primary Web2 shortcomings:

- **Privacy and Security** – by using the most up-to-date cryptographic technologies to build a better web, we can ensure Internet users can keep their information private, away from hackers, companies, and anyone else who might want to use it.
- **Decentralized Storage** – small files can be broken down into smaller chunks and each chunk encrypted and stored elsewhere. Protocols such as the IPFS Network are designed so that breaching them would require multiple devices worldwide being hacked simultaneously, and each device would have its own separate security.
- **Identity and Reputation** – if you are wondering how online trust and reputation can be dealt with, considering all the anonymity in place, you wouldn't be

alone. Already, we have digital identities consisting of uploaded data, but, right now, we have no control or ownership over that data. That will change with Web 3.

The State of Web 3

Right now, technologies aimed at making all this possible are already in development. Take the Databox Project as an example. The project aims to develop an open-source device used to store your personal data locally, keeping it away from tech companies who use it for their own purposes. Another project called Zeronet offers an alternative to traditional web hosting – hosting is done by a network of computers rather than one central server and with the same cryptographic protection that Bitcoin uses.

Decentralized peer-to-peer networks, such as IPFS and Ethereum, are used to build DApps, which are Web 3 applications. Rather than a company running these networks, the users build, operate, and maintain them.

Lastly, a decentralized YouTube, called DTube, is already hosting video using the blockchain as its payment and database system.

The real revolution is just beginning, and, over time, the way we build Web 3 apps will change as the surrounding infrastructure evolves. The key point is that we are already building these apps, and Web 3 is a reality, not just a pipedream.

This book will help you understand exactly what Web 3 is, how it works, why we need it, and how to build a Web 3 app. We will also look at the differences between the Web 2 and Web 3 architecture, what Web 3 offers now and what the future will bring, and how it is set to change the way we live our lives forever.

Chapter 1: Why Do We Need a New Internet?

That's an excellent question. Doesn't the Internet we have now work just fine? Well, yes, but a couple of important properties are missing:

1. No "state" is held independently of the trusted operators, and
2. There is no native mechanism for transferring state.

Why is this important?

The lack of state is a result of the simplicity of the current protocols used to build the web, like SMTP and HTTP. Right now, if you queried a node (a connected device) about its state or history, it couldn't tell you. This would be like a user opening the Internet for the first time, using a new browser with no browsing history, no history, no bookmarks, auto-complete disabled, and no saved settings. This would happen every time you used the Internet, and you would be forced to put in your user information for every service, every single time. You would have to download your favorite apps or open your favorite websites from scratch every time, leaving you with an inefficient, almost unusable system.

However, state represents value and is a critical part of developing services and applications, and two important developments have fixed the state drawback issue:

- The invention of cookies –allows JavaScript-based web applications to preserve state on individual local devices. However, cookies come with their own problems – the user doesn't create them. Instead, this is done by the service providers, meaning the user doesn't

control which providers give them state or can access state.
- Centralized service providers hold user state on their machines. Right now, Google, Facebook, Twitter, and other large web companies hold state, which means they also have sole access to the value billions of users create. There isn't too much wrong with that because users also benefit from the value and services created by those tech giants. However, it is known that these companies benefit far more from the Internet than the public.

The second property missing from today's Internet is the lack of a state transfer mechanism, which stems partly from the first property. If state cannot be held, along with the created value, it can't be transferred. Today's modern finance and economic development is highly dependent on transferring value efficiently and easily, and any improvement in that will provide positive benefits. Because we can already transfer huge amounts of information, new services and businesses can benefit from the huge potential offered. However, if businesses cannot trace value easily, they must look for alternative methods to profit from their services.

That's why the Internet's prevailing business model has become advertising. Advertising businesses can easily store state for billions of users and transmit them efficiently. Again, this isn't wrong per se, but it does create a three-fold problem:

1. An intermediary facilitates every advertising transaction, and they are the ones who profit from them
2. Advertising is more favorable for long-established businesses, so newly created businesses are at an immediate disadvantage, which limits growth potential for the economy

3. Rich advertising economies rely heavily on user data to feed their ad models, creating poor UX and misaligned user incentives.

The Internet Needs Direction

As it stands, the Internet is one of the largest technological developments. However, it is nothing more than a jumble of pipes that don't care what we humans do. It's down to humans to point those pipes in the right direction, and, as time has passed, it has become increasingly obvious that the current direction cannot benefit anyone other than those who already benefit from it. Over the next couple of decades, we need to facilitate two things to point the Internet in a better direction:

1. Allowing any participant to create native economic value
2. The ability to transfer that value to any participant

Thanks to Satoshi Nakamoto, we have the blockchain, and that gives us the perfect way to allow every network participant to hold state and transfer it in a digital format. Many entrepreneurs and developers have begun building on this state layer and, with open-source platforms like Ethereum, this is being made easier as each day passes. The more people are aware of how these capabilities benefit them, the more they sound the warning bell, demanding an open and fairer Internet for all, and that is where Web 3 enters the picture.

Chapter 2: What Is Web 3?

In the last chapter, we learned that the Internet we use today is stateless, which means users cannot hold their state and natively transfer it. When Bitcoin came out, it brought the blockchain, allowing us to hold state digitally and natively. Those using the blockchain ecosystem have begun referring to this capability as Web 3 and, although it is still relatively new, we are already beginning to see how it can benefit us.

We'll discuss all that later, but this chapter will look at how today's Internet stack looks and what it might look like in the future.

The Internet framework is, essentially, a system of layers. Those layers begin at the top and are built downwards. The colors you see in the image above show module compatibility in the layers. For example, Crypto Goods (yellow) are compatible with EVM (the blue to yellow) but are not compatible with Bitcoin Script (the green to red).

EVM has compatibility with the Ethereum blockchain (blue) but isn't compatible with the green Bitcoin Blockchain. This lets us add a Crypto Good to the framework in the future that will have compatibility with the Bitcoin Script, thus allowing it to be recorded in the Bitcoin Blockchain – note that this is not really likely because of the technical challenges involved. However, it does illustrate that we need modularity like this to ensure Web 3 is robust – we should not need to rewrite everything that comes below a layer we want to upgrade.

You should also note that, while each layer's modules may look different in a few years, the layers are comprehensive and cover everything needed to create and run Web 3.

Let's have a look at what each layer does.

State Layer

The state is responsible for preserving the state of everything that happens beneath it. Only the blockchain infrastructure provides this layer, and all users can participate as long as they abide by the preferred network's rules. The goal for a successful network is to provide a default infrastructure, reliable and much like the DNS providers of today's Internet. When they work as they are meant to, 99% of the time, they are invisible, but everyone suffers when they don't work.

The State layer can be public or private (permissioned). It could be argued that state is a universal and singular truth by default, and when you create a private layer, it's almost like creating a parallel universe.

From this point on, all layers are built on the layers below or are compatible with them.

Computation Layer

When we use software, it lets us pass instructions to computers, and the Computation layer lets us tell the State layer what we want it to do. However, not every Computation layer will let anything be done, like the Bitcoin Script. This is limited, allowing transaction orders and not much else. On the other end of the spectrum is the EVM (Ethereum Virtual Machine), a full Turing Complete machine. This means EVM-supported State layers can do complex computations.

Application and blockchain developers need to determine which Computation layer they will use very carefully. Their choice determines the blockchain an application can run on. For example, an application that has been compiled to EVM cannot run on the Bitcoin blockchain, but it can run on the Ethereum blockchain. The Ethereum Foundation is now working on changing the default Ethereum Computation layer to eWASM, a different technology based on WASM (WebAssembly.) And State Layer projects like Dfinity are also planning to move to WASM compatibility, meaning an application that was compiled to eWASM could, in theory, work on Dfinity and Ethereum blockchains or any other WASM-compatible blockchain.

Component Layer

When the State and Computation layers are combined, it results in more design space for new digital values types (programmable money.) Already, we are beginning to see developers experiment, and some of their implementations have huge potential, allowing us to imagine sub-economies being built entirely on a specific component.

The Computation layer is where components are built, and they reuse the standard templates for smart contracts. The component's creator must issue their new smart contracts on the State layer, and examples of the components can be seen below:

- **Native Currency** – A core part of the public blockchain, this provides participants with the right to pay and receive a service from the blockchain. This is a form of transaction, such as Ether or Bitcoin.
- **Crypto Assets** – These are fungible assets with basic functionality sets and associated metadata. They were responsible for the ICO boom because anyone can essentially create digital money. Beyond that, other asset types can be digitized, such as bonds, stocks, and ownership rights, and ERC-20 is the most common standard.

- **Crypto Goods** – These are non-fungible assets with basic functionality sets and rich metadata, and they are also known as NFTs (Non-Fungible Tokens) or crypt collectibles. Unique goods, like access rights, game assets, rights, and collectible items can be digitized, and ERC-721 is the most common standard.
- **Identity** – This is a self-sovereign container designed to hold identity information. It doesn't provide much good information about what it can identify, but we can associate claims with the container. These claims can come from all over the place, such as trusted parties or governments. ERC-725 and ERC-735 are the leading proposals, and uPort also provides protocol proposals. One of the most relevant identifier types is ENS (Ethereum Naming Service).
- **Stablecoins** – These are crypto assets with stable values and are pegged against something like the USD value.

Protocol Layer

Once we have created the Components on the State layer, they must be brought to life. Some functions are common to these components' lifecycles, a fundamental part and responsible for standardizing them. These functions are required to talk the same language and are made more efficient by the network effects. Essentially, these protocols allow healthy markets to be formed for the components, similar to the real world but larger, cheaper, and way more efficient.

Over time, some protocols have begun gaining traction, taking the form of smart contracts the development team deploys. These smart contracts are called by the application that needs the right function to be deployed on a component:

- **Trading** – A component must be tradable to have values. Protocols allow for wallet-to-wallet asset trading in a trustless manner. You must understand the difference between "relayers" and "decentralized exchanges" – the latter take assets on a smart contract into their custody. When a trade is facilitated through trading protocols, they don't take custody of the traded assets.
- **Lending** – This increases any asset's efficiency, as it allows for returns on the investment where they might otherwise have been zero. Standard lending protocols enable someone in the US to lend money to someone else in a different country using their smartphones.
- **Derivatives** – This is one of the largest markets worldwide, with an estimated global value of approximately $1.2 quadrillion. When derivatives are built as a protocol, trustless markets can be formed for native components on the State layer.

Scalability/Transfer Layer

The scalability issues surrounding the blockchain are well-known. The Bitcoin blockchain can only process seven transactions per second, while Ethereum can process fifteen. However, although much debate has taken place on whether the blockchains should do something to facilitate thousands per second, it's now widely accepted that Layer-2 scalability, a separate layer for state transfer, is needed to support the topology. All scalability solutions have got to be compatible with the blockchain's computation layer. Here are some of the proposals on how this could be done:

- **Payment Channels** – Only allows for a specified native currency to be transferred via verifiable signatures attached on the State layer to each

transaction. However, funds are required to be deposited in case of disputes.
- **State Channels** – Allows any state to be transferred via verifiable signatures attached on the State layer to the transaction. Again, funds must be deposited in case of disputes.
- **Side Chains** – Allows any state to be transferred by other blockchains compatible with the main blockchain. The side chain must be able to converse with the main blockchains computation layer, and funds must be deposited in case of disputes. The side chain can be privately or centrally managed.

We're on the fifth layer, and you should now be able to see how the modular nature of the stack lets developers have independence from some of the design choices on the lower levels, such as choosing the right blockchain to build their application on.

User Control Layer

Until now, it has not been possible for average users to make use of any created functionality unless they use a command-line interface to talk to the Computation layer. That changes with this layer, as its main function is to manage users' keys and sign the transactions on the State layer. Those transactions change a user's account state and are a core part of our interaction with Web 3 applications.

We can choose from two types of wallets:

- **Hosted** – Crypto exchanges like Coinbase made these popular as they manage a user's funds through control of a small set of State layer balances. Users' funds may be pooled, and individual states can be managed externally to the State layer. This would probably only

be economic if monetary value were the only consideration but, with the huge increase in states Web 3 applications will bring, it becomes more difficult.
- **User-Controlled** – These are more flexible, providing a direct way of consuming the complex operations Web 3 makes possible. A wallet is made user-controlled by the private keys being taken into local custody and each transaction locally signed. The software will not replicate the private keys in a way that makes it easy for transactions to be submitted by a third party.

This point is the ultimate point for all the underlying layers. That means all available functionality to any application accessed via the layer must be exposed, usually via front-end libraries, which we'll dig into a bit deeper in the next chapter.

Application Layer

As with today's Internet, most Web 3 activity will be via applications built on the layers below this one. For example, users can realize the value in Crypto Goods because the functionality comes via applications that consume the goods. Web 3 apps don't have the same requirements or properties as traditional applications and are usually referred to as DApps, or decentralized apps. In time, these must be easily distinguishable from the traditional apps, especially if millions of users will be using them.

However, the functionalities decentralization enables are why DApps are powerful and why usage numbers are expected to go way beyond today's Internet, especially as the stack grows in maturity. Already, we see developers creating cutting-edge use cases, and users are already responding to those cases by placing their money where they see the most value.

- **Fundraising** – Already, nearly $20 billion has been raised, with more than 720,000 unique accounts, and more than 8,000 companies have received some form of investment. Sure, there has been fraud, but this is by far the most popular category, based on how many unique accounts have participated. Its attraction continues growing, as we can see evidenced by the number of new fundraising platforms facilitating ICOs subject to being regulated.
- **Trading Platforms** – A traditional trading platform acts as a hosted wallet. It is an intermediary between the user and the State layer, while Web 3 applications leave the user controlling their own funds. The UX benefits are also much better. While projects are already working on getting around the technical challenges, this area has already picked up in terms of users.
- **Games and Collectibles** – Between $50 and 100 million has already been raised with more than 60,000 new accounts owing crypto goods. Although this is behind fundraising, because some games can interact with crypto goods, they offer the gaming market serious potential.

Chapter 3: How Web 3 Works

Over the last couple of chapters, we have discussed the stateless entity that is today's Internet, how participants cannot hold or transfer their state natively to another. When blockchains were introduced, we got a stateful Internet of computers which is now being called Web 3.

This new Internet gives us an extra layer of infrastructure that applications can interact with, not to mention a whole slew of new client requirements and functionalities. New UX concepts must be learned if we are to use these applications efficiently. That means Web 3 application architecture brings us extra elements over Web 2 and provides new tools and building blocks for developers to use.

Web 2 vs. Web 3 Architecture

Perhaps the simplest way of looking at Web 2 architecture is that it contains a suite of servers that provide logic, content, and client software, normally a self-contained app or a browser, and all of this is controlled by one entity. This entity would have the only control over who could access the logic and content on the servers and hold a record of what is owned by who and how long the content is live. Across the history of the Internet, we can see tons of examples of how companies have changed user rules or even stopped providing a service. The users can do nothing about it, losing all the value they created.

With Web 3 architecture, a universal State layer allows us to leverage what it enables by allowing the following:

1. It allows applications to put all or some of their logic and content on a public blockchain. That means, unlike

Web 2, the logic and content are public, and anyone can access them.

2. It also users to have direct control of their logic and content. Where Web 2 users need an account or a privileged API key to interact with content on a blockchain, Web 3 users can do it without.

Two pieces of key infrastructure enable Web 3 apps to enable this:

- **Wallets** – modern wallets are more than just a Web 3 stack User Control layer. They allow us to interact with the client frontend, providing a smooth user experience. Applications use standard libraries, of which web3.js is the most popular, to send a request to the wallet. An example of this could be a request for payment, requesting that the user confirm the wallet is authorized to send the payment to the applicant. Once the user has accepted, two things will happen. First, the wallet tells the frontend what has happened, so a Payment Submitted screen can be shown, and, second, an RPC call is made by the wallet to the server, submitting the transaction to the blockchain. This leads us to the second bit of architecture.

- **Blockchain Node** – two types of agents are constantly monitoring the blockchain and engaging with it - miners and nodes. The miners maintain the blockchain directly and run it, while nodes monitor the transactions and submit them to the blockchain. Think of them as being similar to an ISP vs. a Cloud service provider, such as AWS. In much the same way as applications run their backends using AWS services, node providers do the same thing with a blockchain node. When a wallet requests to submit transactions or queries certain State information, the mode provider is called. An application's server may also interact with the providers to keep app logic updated, and this, too, is done by making an RPC call.

What Developers Should Know

While developers have the coding know-how to get to grips with Web 3, there are some other things they will need to know:

Tools and Frameworks

All developers know the best tools and frameworks to use in a given job, and they must be proficient at using them. Web 3 may still be in early development, but we now have a series of usable tools developers can use to get to an MVP stage and iterate fast. We can clearly see this on Ethereum, where an incredibly active community has ensured developers are flocking to the platform in huge numbers.

I won't dig too deeply into the available tools, but you should know the best ones to start with:

Design Choices

- **What to Decentralize** – this is a new choice and an important one. Early developers have set themselves targets to get as much decentralized as possible and get it all on the blockchain. However, our blockchains are quite slow and expensive to run at the moment, so decentralizing at scale is not likely to happen very fast. One of the first DApps that trialed keeping some things decentralized was CryptoKitties. For example, they don't make breeding logic available publicly. While they have been criticized for their choice, users still spend vast amounts of money purchasing cats bred using that logic. Another example is Gods Unchained, a game hosted on a cloud infrastructure but tracking asset ownership on the State layer.

DApps will take different decentralization approaches, but a First Principles approach method would be the adoption of a "minimally viable public state." Let's say you are developing a game where participants can own assets. In that case, the blockchain would store the ownership. If you were developing a prediction market, the blockchain should be responsible for storing the reporting and market payout. Users will only gain value from your application if they have ownership of your application's key activities.

- **Web Apps vs. Native Apps** – this is a decades-old approach yet, with a Web 3 application, it takes on a whole new form. Most of today's DApps are web applications for two reasons – the user is not required to download an app every time and can use the app without the need for a new wallet each time. There aren't many native DApps, and they all request users create new wallets, not really the best experience for the user. We can easily see how this will not be feasible in the future. Users will not want to maintain keys for multiple wallets, but there will soon be better ways of enabling a native app to get past this. For the moment, web apps are easier to use.
- **Desktop vs. Mobile** – in terms of Web 3, this isn't about picking one or the other. It's about determining how your users will use your DApp on both of them. On the desktop, MetaMask or other similar Chrome extensions are how most interaction with DApps is done. While a new extension must be downloaded, it

still allows the user the ability to interact with a familiar browser interface.

Extensions are not possible on mobiles, at least not on iOS, which is why Wallet apps have browsers in the app. Once the user is in the browser view, their experience is the same as on the desktop.

Other Challenges

Right now, these challenges don't have a solution:

- **Who Pays for the Gas?** – Ethereum DApps require users to pay the transaction costs, which are known as gas on the Ethereum blockchain. Should millions of native people not involved in crypto use Web 3 applications in the future, this simply won't be possible. There are some solutions, only theoretical at this stage, but very few are anywhere near practical, and none are functional at the time of writing.
- **App-Specific Accounts?** – Web 3 offers an exciting application – universal identity. Right now, we don't have too many identify solutions that work, so some DApps still require users to create accounts to allow their app activity to be associated with an identity. That's pretty much how Web 2 does things but, once a decentralized working solution is in place, how would a DApp treat this?

These are questions that will be answered as Web 3 development progresses. And as that development moves on, the way we build Web 3 apps will also evolve. However, the key thing right now is those apps already built and in use.

In the next chapter, we'll take a look at what decentralized apps are and how to build one.

Chapter 4: Building a DApp

Shortly, we will look at how to build a DApp but first, an overview of all you need to know.

What Are DApps?

The standard apps that you use today on your desktop or mobile, like Facebook, Twitter, Uber, etc., run on a system that one organization owns and operates. That organization has total authority over that app and the way it runs. While there may be many users on the frontend, a single organization controls the backend.

DApps, or Decentralized Applications, run on a blockchain network or a P2P network. Examples of applications on computers in a P2P (Peer-to-Peer) network are Popcorn Time, Tor, and BitTorrent, where many participants are feeding or seeding content, consuming it, or doing it all simultaneously.

In the cryptocurrency context, a DApp uses a blockchain network. The environment is open-source, public, decentralized, and not interfered with or controlled by a single organization or authority.

For example, suppose a DApp developer created an app similar to Twitter. In that case, they could place it on the blockchain, allowing any user to publish messages which could not be deleted once posted – not even by the app developer.

What Is Ethereum?

Ethereum is a blockchain technology implementation capable of running smart contracts. The EVM (Ethereum Virtual Machine) is known as a Turing complete machine, and arbitrary computation can be run directly on the blockchain network. Bitcoin is limited in its commands, but an Ethereum contract lets a developer specify the exact transactions that may be performed on the contract. You could think of a simple smart contract as being a Finite State Machine with custom transitions defined.

What Is a Smart Contract?

A smart contract allows blockchain users to exchange property and money or do some other actions among a user group, such as casting a vote without the need for a central authority. The Ethereum platform uses the Solidity language to define smart contracts.

What Is JSON-RPC?

It is a Remote Procedure Call (RPC) protocol, light-weight and stateless, that uses JSON for its payload. Where RESTful APIs are centered on resources, RPC APIs are procedural and can be coupled tighter than RESTful APIs.

Frontend apps use JSON-RPC to communicate with Ethereum, and the JSON-RPC spec is used to build the compatible API (Web 3) and the bindings. All decentralized apps must be built using a Web 3 SDK.

Let's Build a DApp

Now you understand a little more about Ethereum DApps, let's look at how to build one. We're using the Truffle Framework, which has the tools and the boilerplate code we need to scaffold Ethereum DApps but, before we get down to it, let's look at what we need to consider:

- **Is there a UI in the DApp?** Yes. The only time a DApp won't have a UI is when it is an automated process. Most DApps have some UI component since we usually need to interact with the Ethereum network or smart contract. If your DApp is browser-based, the UI is built in JavaScript. We're using React, as it is a popular SPA framework.

- **Has your Smart Contract been designed?** This is how the DApp's transitions and rules are defined and is what runs in the EVM. Try not to put any unnecessary logic into your contracts as it can prove expensive to run the computation in terms of gas. We will use a simple contract provided by Truffle, SimpleStorage, which stores storedData (an unsigned integer) and gives us a getter and setter.

```
pragma solidity ^0.4.18;

contract SimpleStorage {
   uint storedData;

   function set(uint x) public {
      storedData = x;
   }

   function get() public view returns (uint) {
      return storedData;
   }
}
```

- **What about the test environment?** Any transactions you write into an Ethereum contract cost gas to compute, so you should have a test network to get around this. Ethereum does provide official networks, but you can use the local test environment in Truffle.

Step By Step

You can follow these instructions practically on your computer, or you can just read through them to get an idea of how it all works.

1. **Install the Truffle Framework**

```
npm install -g truffle
```

The -g flag is used to ensure the framework can be used for other projects.

2. **Generate Boilerplate**

```
truffle unbox react
```

Boilerplates are called boxes in Truffle, and the React boilerplate is based on the Facebook boilerplate, create-react-app.

A set of folders and files should now be generated, and there are a few specific ones to consider:

- **src/ -** the folder that stores the react code
- **contracts/ -** the folder that stores Solidity-based smart contracts. Here, you will find a file called SimpleStorage.sol
- **migrations/ -** the scripts used to manage contract deployment to the Ethereum network

- **public/** - here, you will find a file called index.html, which is the entry point for injecting the react app.

3. **Start Development Environment**

```
truffle develop
```

Two things will be started with this command – the Ethereum Node emulator starts at http://127.0.0.1:9545, creating ten test accounts, each seed with 100 ether. Second, the truffle command-line prompt is started.

4. **Compiling the Contracts**

```
compile
```

Your Solidity contracts will be compiled into JSON artifacts, including the Ethereum Virtual Machine (=EVM) bytecode. Your compiled contracts are stored in the folder called build/contracts.

5. **Deploying your Contracts**

```
migrate
```

This command deploys your contracts to the emulated network – we can deploy our contracts onto the real network at a later time by modifying a file called truffle-config.js.

6. **Trial Run**

Now you can try running the DApp in your browser.

```
npm run start
```

However, right now, it has little interaction with Ethereum, so we need to add some. Before we do that, we must connect to an Ethereum network – this is done with the web3 object and setting the preferred provider.

7. Modifying the DApp Code

App.js references the web3 object found in the React lifecycle method called componentWillMount(), which is stored in the local state. A local version of the contract is also instantiated:

```
getWeb3
.then(results => {
  this.setState({
    web3: results.web3
  })


  // Instantiate contract once web3 provided.
  this.instantiateContract()
})
.catch(() => {
  console.log('Error finding web3.')
})
```

Now, we add a small form:

```
<form className="pure-form pure-form-stacked">
   <fieldset>
      <label htmlFor="storage">Storage Amount</label>
```

```
      <input id="storage" type="number"
ref={c => { this.storageAmountInput = c
}} />

      <button

         className="pure-button"

         onClick={(e) => {

           e.preventDefault();

           this.addToSimpleStorage()

         }}

      >

         Set Storage

      </button>

   </fieldset>

</form>
```

This form allows users set the value to be stored in our SimpleStorage contract. Below you can see the button's action handler:

```
addToSimpleStorage() {

   if (this.state.simpleStorageInstance &&
this.state.accounts) {

      const value =
this.storageAmountInput.value;
```

```js
      this.state.simpleStorageInstance.set(value, {from: this.state.accounts[0]})
        .then((result) => {
          return this.state.simpleStorageInstance.get.call(this.state.accounts[0])
        }).then((result) => {
          this.setState(prevState => ({
            ...prevState,
            storageValue: result.c[0]
          }));
        }).catch((err) => {
          console.log('error');
          console.log(err);
        });
    } else {
      this.setState(prevState => ({
        ...prevState,
        error: new Error('simple storage instance not loaded')
      }))
    }
```

```
        }
```

The handler provides the SimpleStorage instantiated contract and the local state accounts. Next, storageValue must be set with the value we get from the HTML form.

That's the app created but, before we move on, you should be aware that the simpleStorage contract set method is triggered by simpleStorageInstance.set

8. **Running the DApp**

```
npm run start
```

A smart contract's storage value can also be set and stored on the blockchain.

Setting up API Monitoring

Because DApps don't have centralized servers, there are none to install any monitoring tools when you deploy your app in production. To ensure interactions between the contract and network are monitored, we would need a monitoring solution with support for DApps.

One of the most popular is called Moesif, offering support as a compatible API to provide analytics and monitoring.

Moesif captures the data from the API call from the client-side using a browser SDK. In turn, this can help with monitoring, debugging and inform you if any anomalies are found.

We're using moesif-browser.js.

1. Create your Moesif account using the linked website – this will provide you with an application ID.

2. Go to public/index.html and add the following code:

```
<script src="//unpkg.com/moesif-browser-js@1.2.0/moesif.min.js"></script>
<script type="text/javascript">
var options = {
   applicationId: 'The application id you have on Moesif'
   // additional option to be added here.
};


// for options see below.
moesif.init(options);


// the data capturing will be started with this command.
moesif.start();
</script>
```

3. Reload the DApp

Moesif detects Ethereum Web 3 calls automatically and tracks them. You can verify the captured events by going to the event stream in your Moesif account.

That really is all there is to creating and running a simple DApp, and this gives you a sound basis for building your knowledge to create more complex contracts.

Chapter 5: The Real Differences between Web 2 and Web 3

Web 2 is the Internet we are all familiar with right now, an Internet controlled by companies who happily provide you with a service, so long as you hand over your personal details into their custody, to do with what they want. Web 3, in Ethereum's context, is a system of decentralized apps and computers running on the blockchain. These apps allow you to take part without having your personal data monetized by a third party.

Here's a brief look at the benefits, the reasons why Web 3 developers opt to build DApps using the decentralization offered by Ethereum:

- Anyone participating on the network automatically has permission to use a service. Put simply, you don't need permission – if you're on it, you have it.
- No one can stop you from using a service
- The native token, Eth, is where the payments are built-in
- Ethereum is classed as Turing Complete – you can program just about anything you want.

The Practical Comparisons

WEB 2	WEB 3
Twitter may censor a tweet or account whenever they want, without prior warning or permission	Web 3 tweets and accounts could not be censored because there is no central control – it's all decentralized
A payment service can opt not	Web 3 payment apps don't ask

to allow payments for some types of work	for any personal information, and they can't stop payments
Gig-economy app servers may go down without warning, affecting income for the workers	Web 3 servers cannot go down as their backend is made up of a decentralized network of thousands of computers

However, these show you just the main differences between Web 2 and Web 3 services – it doesn't automatically follow that every service must be turned into a DApp.

Web 3 Limitations

Being so new, Web 3 does still have some limitations at the moment:

- **Scalability** – Web 3 transactions tend to be much slower, and that's down to the decentralization aspect. Miners must process changes to state, such as a payment, and those changes are then propagated through the entire network.
- **UX** – when you interact with a Web 3 app, it can take extra software, steps, and education. Right now, this is one of the biggest things that will get in the way of adoption.
- **Cost** – successful DApps only put small parts of their code into the blockchain to keep the cost down.

Centralization vs. Decentralization

To help you understand the real differences between Web 2 and Web 3, it would help to understand the difference between centralization and decentralization in terms of digital networks:

Centralized Systems	Decentralized systems
The network diameter is low, as all participants connect to one centralized authority. Information can be quickly propagated because a centralized authority controls and handles it, using vast amounts of computation resources.	The network diameter is much larger as participants are not connected to a central authority but a decentralized network. It can take much longer for information to get from one side of the network to the other.
Tends to offer higher performance, evidenced by fewer computational resources being expended and much higher throughput. Centralized systems can also be implemented easier.	Tend to offer lower performance because more computational resources are needed, and the throughput is lower. They are also much harder to implement.
Should there be a data conflict, it is easy and clear to resolve it because the central authority is the ultimate decider.	Protocols, which are often quite complex, are required to resolve disputes, especially where peers submit conflicting statements about the state of the data participants should be synchronized on.
It has one single point of failure – a hacker can target the central authority and take the network down, as we have seen numerous times in the past.	There is no single point of failure. Even if the majority of participants were hacked and taken down, the network would still operate.
Coordination between the	Coordination isn't easy

participants on the network is easy, and the central authority handles everything. The central authority has the power to compel participants to adopt updates with little to no friction.	because no one agent has the overall say in decisions made at the network level, or about protocol upgrades, and so on. Worst case, the network can fracture when protocol changes are the subject of disagreement among the network participants.
The central authority has the power to censor any data, which can result in parts of the network being stopped from accessing or interacting with the remainder.	Censorship isn't quite so easy because information can be propagated in multiple ways across the network.
A central authority controls all network participation	Anyone can take part, and no one can stop you. In an ideal world, participation costs would be kept very low.

NOTE

These are only generalizations, and they may not be true for all networks. Also worth remembering is that the degree of centralization or decentralization is firmly on a spectrum – no network can be entirely decentralized or centralized.

Chapter 6: The Main Features of Web 3

In the late 1990s, the Internet as we know it today started to become more widely adopted and, since then, it has become deeply intertwined with our lives. We don't see what goes on behind the scenes; an ecosystem made up of protocols, technologies, and networks, all combining to make the Internet function and all constantly in a state of flux. In the same way, every user experiences the Internet differently, in constantly changing ways.

Web 3 is designed to change that. It's the next revolution of the Internet, defined by user sovereignty and decentralization. To understand Web 3 and its implications, you need to see it in its place in the evolution of the Internet:

- **Web 1** – This was the first iteration of the Internet, mostly made up of static HTML pages that displayed data we couldn't interact with, centrally sourced data. Because of this, most users were nothing more than content consumers. Emails and basic messaging were the most advanced forms of digital communication. However, although these limitations were there, Web 1 soon revolutionized how we connected and exchanged information. In short, Web 1 brought us a brand new digital world that sucked us in and has kept us almost permanently captivated.
- **Web 2** – The Internet began evolving in the 2000s into the digital landscape we are more familiar with today. Web 2 brought us better social experiences online, and network effects, multidirectional data flow, and crowdsourced content brought about new business models. Where Web 1 allowed for better presentation and consummation of data, Web 2 opened the door to a

personalized online experience, using user interactions with responsive, dynamic algorithms.

Web 2 may give more users the chance to interact and participate in creating web content, but it isn't without its issues – several of them, to be fair. As we've already made clear, the Internet is controlled by a small number of tech giants, companies who act as gatekeepers, controlling all our personal information and what we can see and do on the web. You might think you are using an open system, but these companies track you, track your data, store it and do what they want with it. As programmatic advertising grows, this will just get worse.

If that weren't enough, the current model is largely reliant on centralized protocols and servers for its operations, and that means there are central failure points, points that hackers can target and bring the network to its knees. These days, people are concerned about keeping their data safe and their online identity hidden, which has brought about the sift to the next generation of the Internet.

The Shift to Web 3

Web 3 has been designed to resolve the issues with the Internet we use today. However, its decentralized nature means that its development is also not overseen by any one authority. Rather, an assortment of non-profit organizations, private businesses, and individuals are responsible for progress, approaching development in multiple ways. For example, the Web3 Foundation focuses on the guidelines needed for the Web 3 system. At the same time, ConsenSys Labs help developers build DApps, the applications that are likely to be the primary ones on Web 3.

While all these individuals and teams of developers have different strategies and approaches, most are trying to create frameworks or apps that will service the new Internet on the blockchain, with distributed ledger technology that provides solutions to most of the problems plaguing Web 2. Those frameworks and apps will be deployable in ways that connect and augment other tech. Perhaps the most specific aspect is the blockchain, essential to Web 3 for several reasons:

- **It is open** – since Satoshi Nakamoto introduced the blockchain concept in his Bitcoin whitepaper, the technology has gained definition as an open-source, collaborative ethos, converting accessibility, community governance, and equitability from concepts into real protocols and web services. While private blockchains may attract a small number of use cases, most proponents believe the true potential of the blockchain lies in the public blockchains with their transparency in data records and transactions.

- **It is trustless** – not only are blockchain records transparent, but they are also resistant to censorship and immutable. Smart contracts dictate the rules that govern how a blockchain ledger stores and executes transactions, along with other protocols, which means users can rely on the network performance our output validity without needing to trust any other person or entity on the network. The result is that blockchain technology mitigates operational opacity risks, along with the risks of selectively enforced rules, providing a decentralized way of securing data and transactions.

- **It is permissionless** – Web 3 can succeed only if users can interact without needing third-party intermediaries and central authorities. To achieve this, the decentralized consensus mechanisms and the cryptography in the blockchain technology enable flexible and secure information and value transfers without needing authorization from third parties.

Several blockchain projects are currently working on getting Web 3 established, and Ethereum is the current pack leader as far as scope and user adoption go. However, Web 3 aims to enable a collaborative, decentralized internet, which means those projects should be seen as collective rather than individual teams racing to be the winner.

The Web 3 Architecture

The architecture underlying Web 3 hasn't yet been established, but there is still a consensus on the characteristics Web 3 will feature:

- **A Semantic Web** – part of the underlying operational model is that Web 3 should analyze a broad spectrum of digital content and act on it. To do this, complex associations must be formed between user behavior, web services, and other contextual data. A breakthrough like this enables a never-before-seen level of connectivity between data, a significant difference from how the current model focuses almost entirely on structured numerical values and keywords. The semantic web is designed to ensure Internet data is machine-readable, which will make it far more efficient and effective than it is now.

- **Artificial Intelligence** – advanced Artificial Intelligence will enable the semantic web. The software will be able to decrypt natural language and understand the users' intentions. As such, Web 3 is expected to give us user-centric interaction, a more intuitive experience than the current Internet, which still relies largely on user inputs. The AI processes will also play a huge role in maintaining Web 3's content ecosystem by keeping reliable information separate from fraudulent or low-quality content.

- **Visual Immersion** – the technology we use today provides us with plenty of VR (virtual reality) and AR (augmented reality) experiences. Web 3 will take things further with VR technologies and 3D graphics used in ways we never thought possible, blurring the boundaries between the digital and physical worlds. Physical objects will be rendered in the digital realm, and the digital objects in the physical realm, providing new ways of interacting with services and products and displaying or retrieving information.

- **Secure, Ubiquitous Data** – Web 3 will hasten a brand new era of interconnected IoT devices and interoperability between multiple platforms. As it does, data stored on Web 3 will be applied more flexibly and be more secure than the current way of working. The decentralized network infrastructure will make all this possible, eliminating middlemen who don't add value, removing the risk of centralized servers failing, and giving users control and ownership of their own data. Web 3 may also allow applications to work with multiple devices for software and hardware platforms to interact with no added costs or operational friction.

These innovations are key to Web 3's success, all connected through the blockchain, providing a decentralized network infrastructure that will allow Web 3 to come to fruition.

How Will Web 3 Change Our Lives?

The features mentioned above bring a definition of Web 3 much closer. Here's an example of all these features being brought seamlessly together. In Web 3, let's say you are driving and you have an automotive assistant. You could say something like, "I want to watch an action movie and eat some Chinese food." The in-car assistant has a search engine embedded in it, giving you a personalized response taking your location into account. It will show you the nearest cinema showing an action movie and consult social media reviews to find you the best Chinese restaurant. It may even be able to provide you with a 3D menu from the chosen restaurant.

This might sound like a dream, but it really isn't. In many ways, it is already reality, particularly AI and the semantic web, down to cognitive technology. AI technology uses natural language processing and semantic analysis to extract insights and meaning from unstructured data and web content. Soon, Web 3 will be the overarching Internet, and all of this will be entirely possible.

Chapter 7: Why Web3 Is An Investment Opportunity

We have already covered at length in this book the enormous potential that the Web3 represents for content providers and consumers alike. The Web3 is a complete game-changer, a next-generation Internet with new business models and massive opportunities for consumers to engage in and profit from its growth.

This amazing new field will bring with it a myriad of investment opportunities for prepared and savvy investors who know what to look for. However, contrary to the Web2 where much profit was to be made with choosing the right Dotcom stocks (and avoiding the bad ones), the investment opportunity here is to be found in the token of the most promising and important Web3 crypto-projects.

Crypto-projects in Web3 are primarily to be found at the level of decentralized protocols and infrastructure providers that lay the foundation for the Web3 as outlined in this book.

Moreover, investment opportunities can be found in decentralized file storage providers like its most famous representative FileCoin – currently a Top-50 coin by market capitalization. However, a little research will reveal to the reader that there are dozens of decentralized file storage providers that have arisen to serve the Web3.

Another great investment opportunity are decentralized content delivery networks (CDNs) like Theta. CDNs provide video, audio and other content services close to where the web users is located. Hosted from decentralized data centers and providers all around the world, the loading times and latency for visitors is reduced, ensuring a smooth and optimal browsing experience.

There are numerous other sub-sections of Web3 tokens that are going to arise in the coming weeks and months. We advise readers to keep checking the leading news sources and follow industry leaders in order not to miss out on some of the most amazing investment opportunities of our time.

Chapter 8: 3 Most Promising Web3 Tokens for 2022

In this previous chapter, we discussed about the great investment opportunity the Web3 represents. In this chapter, we want to introduce our personal pick of the 3 most promising Web3 tokens for 2021 and 2022: BitTorrent, LivePeer, Helium.

BitTorrent (BTT)

The BitTorrent protocol has been a game-changing for peer-to-peer file sharing when it was originally released in 2006. Since changing to become a crypto-project with its own native token, BitTorrent has become one resounding success story. The BitTorrent token gained more than 800 % between Q1-Q3 2021 and chances are it still has massive upward potential from here. As the Web3 gains more traction, more and more people will start making use of the BitTorrent clients for distributed file sharing across the world.

The BTT token is currently available for trading at Binance and Coinbase exchange.

LivePeer (LPT)

Livepeer is an Ethereum-based protocol targeted towards video infrastructure providers and streaming applications. It offers an alternative to centralized content distribution networks (CDNs) that pose risks of censorship or a single point of failure. Users can earn LPT tokens for providing bandwidth and resources to the network. Companies buy and pay LPT tokens in order to provide their videos via the network.

The LPT token is currently available for trading at Binance and Coinbase exchange.

Helium (HNT)

Helium is a little-recognized game changer for the telecommunications industry. It utilizes a combination of connected blockchains and tokens that together help to incentivize users and small companies to provide and validate wireless coverage and transfer device data over their network. Basically, Helium uses available and unused bandwidth of its users to offer an alternative, decentralized 5G network that can compete with the big telecommunication providers.

The HNT token is currently available for trading at Binance and Coinbase exchange.

Conclusion

Web 3 is the next evolution of the Internet, the next phase in a continually evolving system. It was designed to help fix existing internet problems and provide us with a human-centric system where personalized interactions are the way ahead. While we don't yet have full details of the underlying architecture, decentralized technology will likely be used to connect and enable the main features.

The future is ours but only if we are willing to take a chance and grasp it firmly in our hands. It is ours if the policymakers are prepared to see that technological and financial laws are not sacred, in the same way that business models are not sacred. If policymakers ditch their laws, their IT industries will likely become outdated, slow, and clunky, and Web 3 will never get adopted. An example is updating laws to ensure people can only spend that country's fiat currency on products and services produced there.

The implications of the blockchain go much deeper than speculating on the Bitcoin price. Content creators will be able to capture much greater value, and economic transactions will become much faster. The Internet will become resistant to censorship, data structures will become more democratic, fundraising much easier, cross-border payments will get easier, and users will control their own identities. For the most part, much of this is already here, but it will become easier to manage and more commonplace

Web 3 is promising us a better, safer world. All we have to do is find the right way to welcome it.

References

"5 Main Features of Web 3.0." *Expert.ai*, 29 Apr. 2020, www.expert.ai/blog/web-3-0/.

B, Tyler. "Web3 for Dummies — a Quick Guide." *Online.io Blockchain Technologies*, 22 Feb. 2020, medium.com/online-io-blockchain-technologies/web3-for-dummies-a-quick-guide-eaddc9fb3ab3.

BetterWorld. "Why We Need Web3." *Medium*, 9 Sept. 2021, brandoncp.medium.com/why-we-need-web3-8e60c42aab37.

Tekisalp, Emre. "Understanding Web 3 — a User Controlled Internet." *Medium*, 30 Aug. 2018, blog.coinbase.com/understanding-web-3-a-user-controlled-internet-a39c21cf83f3.

"The Ultimate Guide to Web3 - What Is Web3?" *Moralis - Build Serverless Web3 Apps*, 16 June 2021, moralis.io/the-ultimate-guide-to-web3-what-is-web3/.

"Web 3.0 Features: A Decentralized and Open Internet." *Gemini*, www.gemini.com/cryptopedia/web-3-0-definition-open-internet-decentralized#section-a-brief-history-of-the-internet.

"Web2 vs Web3." *Ethereum.org*, ethereum.org/en/developers/docs/web2-vs-web3/.

"Web3 - the Decentralized Web." *BlockchainHub*, blockchainhub.net/web3-decentralized-web/.

Printed in Great Britain
by Amazon